KT-226-656

WINTER WARMERS

One Pot

igloobooks

Published in 2016
by Igloo Books Ltd
Cottage Farm
Sywell
NN6 0BJ
www.igloobooks.com

Copyright © 2016 Igloo Books Ltd

All rights reserved. No part of this publication may be
reproduced or transmitted in any form or by any means,
electronic, or mechanical, including photocopying, recording,
or by any information storage and retrieval system,
without permission in writing from the publisher.
The measurements used are approximate.

Food photography and recipe development
© Stockfood, The Food Media Agency

Cover image: © Nadine Greeff / Alamy Stock Photo

Cover designed by Nicholas Gage
Edited by Natalie Baker

LEO002 0916
2 4 6 8 10 9 7 5 3 1
ISBN 978-1-78670-152-7

Printed and manufactured in China

CONTENTS

———— • ————

STARTERS

STEWED ARTICHOKE HEART

SERVES
4

PREPARATION TIME: 10-15 MINUTES
COOKING TIME: 4 HOURS 15 MINUTES

4 globe artichokes, trimmed and halved

30 ml / 1 fl. oz / 2 tbsp olive oil

1 onion, finely chopped

150 g / 5 oz / 1 cup pancetta,
cut into thick strips

500 ml / 18 fl. oz / 2 cups vegetable stock

salt and pepper

METHOD

- Heat a large frying pan over a moderate heat until hot.

- Sauté the pancetta for a few minutes until golden brown in colour on the outside.

- Remove from the pan and transfer to a slow cooker before adding the olive oil to the frying pan.

- Reduce the heat a little and sweat the onion for 5 minutes, stirring occasionally.

- Add the artichoke and cook for a further few minutes before spooning the onion and artichoke into the slow cooker.

- Cover with the stock and cover with a lid.

- Cook on a medium setting for 4 hours until softened.

- Adjust the seasoning to taste before serving.

SALÉ
WITH LENTILS

SERVES
4

PREPARATION TIME: 10 MINUTES
COOKING TIME: 4 HOURS

110 g / 4 oz / ⅔ cup salami, sliced

200 g / 7 oz / 1 cup Puy lentils

500 ml / 18 fl. oz / 2 cups vegetable stock

2 tbsp flat-leaf parsley, finely chopped

½ lemon, juiced

1 bay leaf

METHOD

• Place the lentils, bay leaf and stock in a slow cooker.

• Cook on a low setting for 4 hours until the lentils have absorbed the stock and are tender.

• Drain if necessary and discard the bay leaf.

• Adjust the seasoning to taste with salt, pepper and lemon juice.

• Keep warm on a low setting.

• Preheat the grill to high.

• Grill the salami slices for a minute on both sides until they start to sizzle.

• Remove from the grill and drain on kitchen paper.

• Stir the parsley into the lentils, then ladle into serving bowls using a slotted spoon.

• Sit a couple of slices of salami on top and serve immediately.

TARKA DAL

SERVES
4

PREPARATION TIME: 15 MINUTES
COOKING TIME: 4 HOURS

2 tbsp sunflower oil

1 onion, finely chopped

3 cloves garlic, minced

5 cm / 2 in ginger, peeled and minced

1 green chilli, deseeded and chopped

1 carrot, peeled and finely diced

225 g / 8 oz / 1 ¼ cup tarka dal, soaked in water overnight then drained

500ml / 18 fl. oz / 2 cups vegetable stock

2 tsp ground cumin

2 tsp ground coriander seeds

1 tsp paprika

1 tsp turmeric

1 tsp garam masala

1 tsp amchoor (dried mango powder)

GARNISH

4 sprigs coriander (cilantro)

4 small red chillies

METHOD

- Heat the oil in a large casserole dish set over a medium heat.

- Sweat together the onion, garlic, ginger and chilli with a little salt for 6–7 minutes, stirring occasionally until softened.

- Add the ground spices and stir well, then add the lentils and the stock.

- Stir well then pour into a slow cooker and cook on a low setting for 5 hours until the lentils have absorbed the stock and the mixture is akin to a thick soup.

- Adjust the seasoning to taste then ladle into soup bowls.

- Garnish with the coriander and a small chilli in each bowl.

STEWED CABBAGE

SERVES
4

PREPARATION TIME: 10 MINUTES
COOKING TIME: 4 HOURS 15 MINUTES
2 large Savoy cabbage
30 g / 1 oz / ¼ stick butter
100 g / 4 oz / ⅔ cup pancetta, cubed
250 ml / 9 fl. oz / 1 cup chicken stock
250 ml / 9 fl. oz / 1 cup water
salt and pepper

METHOD

- Cut the cabbages in half; remove the hard inner cores, then cut the halves into large chunks.

- Melt the butter in a large casserole dish over a moderate heat until it stops foaming.

- Add the pancetta and sauté it for 3-4 minutes, stirring occasionally until the pancetta is golden in colour.

- Add the cabbage to the pan and cook, stirring a few times, for 1-2 minutes.

- Spoon the cabbage and pancetta into a slow cooker and cover with the stock.

- Cover with a lid and braise on a medium setting for 4 hours.

- Adjust the seasoning to taste before spooning into serving dishes.

PEA AND POTATO TAGINE

SERVES
4

PREPARATION TIME: 15 MINUTES
COOKING TIME: 4 HOURS 15 MINUTES

2 tbsp olive oil

2 onions, sliced

3 cloves garlic, minced

350 g / 12 oz / 3 cups frozen petit pois, thawed

450 g / 1 lb / 3 cups Maris Piper potatoes, peeled and diced

1 tsp ras el hanout (Moroccan spice blend)

1 tsp ground cumin

1 tsp paprika

750 ml / 1 pint 6 fl. oz / 3 cups vegetables stock

GARNISH
pinch ground cinnamon

METHOD

- Heat the olive oil in a large casserole dish set over a medium heat until hot.

- Sweat the onion and garlic with a little salt for 10 minutes, stirring occasionally until softened.

- Add the potato, peas and ground spices and stir thoroughly.

- Cover with the stock and pour into a slow cooker.

- Cover with a lid and cook on a medium setting for 4 hours until the potato is tender and soft.

- Adjust the seasoning to taste before ladling into serving bowls.

- Garnish with a pinch of ground cinnamon before serving.

FENNEL AND THYME TAGINE

SERVES
4

PREPARATION TIME: 30-45 MINUTES
COOKING TIME: 1 HOUR 15-20 MINUTES

2 tbsp sunflower oil

1 onion, finely chopped

3 cloves of garlic, minced

salt and freshly ground black pepper

1 tsp ground cumin

a pinch of ground cinnamon

a pinch of Cayenne pepper

100 ml / 3 ½ fl. oz / ½ cup tomato ketchup

100 ml / 3 ½ fl. oz / ½ cup cider vinegar

2 tbsp soft dark brown sugar

450 ml / 16 fl. oz / 2 cups chicken stock

METHOD

- Place the fennel bulb halves in a slow cooker and sprinkle with a little water.

- Cover with a lid and cook on a medium setting for 3 hours until softened.

- Remove after 3 hours and pat dry.

- Preheat the oven to 190°C (170°C fan) / 375 F / gas 5.

- Place the fennel in a large mixing bowl and add the oil, sugar and seasoning and toss well.

- Arrange the fennel bulbs with their cut sides facing up on a baking tray. Top with the tomato halves and place a thyme sprig on top.

- Roast for 20-25 minutes until lightly coloured.

- Remove from the oven and transfer to a serving platter.

ROASTED FENNEL

SERVES
4

PREPARATION TIME: 5 MINUTES
COOKING TIME: 3 HOURS 30–35 MINUTES

6 fennel bulbs

30 ml / 1 fl. oz / 2 tbsp olive oil

salt and pepper

GARNISH
sprigs of flowering thyme

METHOD

- Cut the fennel bulbs in half.

- Arrange in a slow cooker and season.

- Cover with a lid and cook on a medium setting for 3 hours until they start to soften.

- Remove from the slow cooker and pat dry.

- Preheat the oven to 190°C (170°C fan) / 375F / gas 5.

- Arrange on a baking tray and drizzle with the olive oil and some more seasoning.

- Roast for 25–30 minutes until lightly coloured.

- Remove from the oven and garnish with the flowering thyme before serving.

RED KIDNEY BEANS WITH PANCETTA

SERVES
4

PREPARATION TIME: 10–15 MINUTES
COOKING TIME: 6 HOURS 10–15 MINUTES

55 ml / 2 fl. oz / ¼ cup olive oil

800 g / 1 lb 12 oz / 4 cups canned red kidney beans, drained

75 g / 3 oz / ½ cup pancetta, cut into large cubes

2 green peppers, de-seeded and quartered

2 onions, peeled and roughly chopped

500 ml / 18 fl. oz / 2 cups vegetable stock

1 tsp smoked paprika

1 bay leaf

salt and pepper

GARNISH
1 large red chilli (chili), de-seeded and finely sliced

METHOD

- Heat a large casserole dish over a moderate heat.

- Sauté the pancetta for 2–3 minutes until coloured all over, then add the peppers and onions to the dish.

- Stir well to combine and cover with a lid.

- Reduce the heat and cook until the vegetables are soft; usually 4–5 minutes.

- Remove the lid then add the kidney beans, stock, bay leaf and paprika.

- Stir well then pour into a slow cooker.

- Cover with a lid and cook on a medium setting for 6 hours until the beans are very soft.

- Remove the lid after 6 hours and discard the bay leaf.

- Adjust the seasoning to taste.

- Spoon into a ceramic serving dish and garnish the top with the sliced red chilli before serving.

COD AND HERB GRATIN

SERVES
4

PREPARATION TIME: 15–20 MINUTES
COOKING TIME: 4 HOURS 50 MINUTES

2 heads cauliflower, prepared into florets

4 cod fillets, pin-boned and diced

500 ml / 18 fl. oz / 2 cups whole milk

1 bay leaf

1 kg / 2 lb 4 oz / 6 ⅔ cups potatoes, peeled and diced

110 g / 4 oz / 1 stick unsalted butter, softened

150 g / 5 oz / 1 ½ cups Parmesan, grated

1 small bunch of tarragon, finely chopped

salt and pepper

GARNISH
2–3 sprigs of thyme

METHOD

• Combine the cod, milk and bay leaf in a slow cooker and cook on a medium setting for 4 hours.

• Strain the cod, making sure you reserve the cooking juice; discard the bay leaf. Place the cooked cod in a bowl and crush. Season with tarragon, salt and pepper to taste.

• Cook the potato and cauliflower in separate saucepans of boiling salted water until tender; the cauliflower will take 5 minutes and the potato will take 20 minutes.

• Drain each vegetable when ready. Once the potato has cooled, mash with the butter and seasoning.

• Crush the cauliflower and fold it through the potato.

• Preheat the oven to 190°C (170°C fan) / 375F / gas 5.

• Spoon the cod into the base of a dish and top with the cauliflower and potato mixture.

• Sprinkle the cheese on top and bake for 15 minutes until golden brown. Garnish with the thyme.

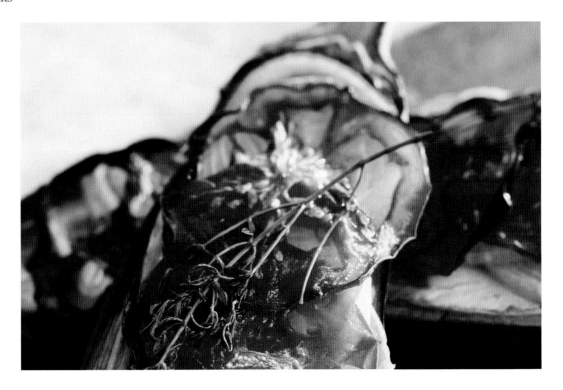

ROASTED AUBERGINES

SERVES
4

PREPARATION TIME: 10 MINUTES
COOKING TIME: 3 HOURS 35 MINUTES

55 ml / 2 fl. oz / ¼ cup olive oil

2 large aubergines (eggplants),
halved lengthways

4 large vine tomatoes, sliced

4 sprigs of thyme

salt and pepper

METHOD

• Arrange the aubergine halves skin-side down in a slow cooker.

• Season the tops and cover with a lid.

• Cook on a medium setting for 3 hours until tender.

• Remove after 3 hours and pat dry.

• Preheat the oven to 200°C (180°C fan) / gas 6.

• Arrange the aubergine halves on a baking tray and drizzle with some of the olive oil.

• Layer the tomato slices on top and drizzle with more olive oil and some seasoning.

• Top each half with a thyme sprig and roast for 20–25 minutes until golden brown on top.

• Remove from the oven and serve on wooden platters.

HONEYED SWEET POTATOES

SERVES
4

PREPARATION TIME: 10 MINUTES
COOKING TIME: 3 HOURS 20 MINUTES

55 ml / 2 fl. oz / ¼ cup olive oil

900 g / 2 lb / 6 cups sweet potatoes, peeled and diced

110 ml / 4 fl. oz / ½ cup honey

100 g / 4 oz / ½ cup golden raisins

1 tsp cloves

salt and pepper

GARNISH

sprigs of coriander (cilantro)

METHOD

- Whisk together the olive oil and honey in a small mixing bowl.

- Coat the sweet potato in the honey and oil mixture and season generously.

- Place in a slow cooker and cover with a lid.

- Cook on a medium setting for 4 hours until tender.

- Remove from the slow cooker and arrange in a roasting tray along with the cloves and raisins.

- Preheat the oven to 200°C (180°C fan) / 400F / gas 6.

- Roast the sweet potatoes for 20 minutes until coloured and golden at the edges.

- Remove from the oven and season a little more before spooning into serving dishes.

- Garnish with the coriander before serving.

23

HEARTY MAINS

BEEF BOURGUIGNON

SERVES
6

PREPARATION TIME: 15 MINUTES

COOKING TIME: 8 HOURS

1 ¾ kg / 4 lb silverside beef, cut into 2 cm cubes

100 g / 4 oz streaky bacon, chopped

30 ml / 1 fl. oz / 2 tbsp vegetable oil or lard

4 cloves, minced

2 large onions, sliced

1 stick celery, sliced

2 carrots, peeled and finely sliced and blanched for 5 minutes

1 tbsp plain (all-purpose) flour

15 ml / 1 tbsp tomato purée

150 ml / ¼ pt / ½ cup beef stock

300 ml / ½ pt / 1 cup heavy red wine

350 g / 12 oz / 1.5 cups mushrooms, brushed and quartered

1 tbsp Dijon mustard

bouquet garni

2 bay leaves

salt and ground black pepper

METHOD

- Heat the oil and fry (sauté) the beef cubes until brown and transfer to the slow cooker.

- Fry the onions, bacon and vegetables for 5 minutes. Stir in the flour and fry for a further minute.

- Pour the stock and wine into the pan, with the herbs and mustard and stir thoroughly. Bring to the boil.

- Transfer all the ingredients to slow cooker.

- Cover and cook on a low setting for 8 hours.

- Taste and adjust seasoning.

CHICKEN WITH COMPOTE

SERVES
4

PREPARATION TIME: 16 MINUTES

COOKING TIME: 6 HOURS

4 chicken breasts, skin on

30 ml / 2 tsp vegetable oil

500 g / 1.5 lb / 1 ¾ cups dried fruit compote from jar

1 medium onion, sliced

2 garlic cloves, minced

60 ml / 2 fl. oz / ¼ cup chicken stock

¼ tsp cinnamon

2 cloves

salt and ground black pepper

METHOD

- Preheat the slow cooker.

- Clean and dry the chicken breasts, season the skin with salt and pepper.

- Heat the oil and fry (sauté) the chicken pieces skin down until brown then turn and fry the underside. Transfer to the slow cooker

- Lightly fry the onions and garlic for 5 minutes, stirring all the time. Combine with the cinnamon and cloves.

- Add the chicken stock and mix in the fruit compote. Bring to a simmer.

- Pour the sauce over the chicken breasts, ensuring they are covered.

- Cover with the lid and cook on a low setting for 6 hours.

LAMB APRICOT TAGINE

SERVES
4

PREPARATION TIME: 20 MINUTES
COOKING TIME: 8 HOURS

800 g / 28 oz / 3 cups lamb shoulder, diced

60 ml / 4 tsp / ¼ cup vegetable oil

4 garlic cloves, minced

2 potatoes, peeled, quartered and blanched

1 tsp ground ginger

3 tsp turmeric and ground cumin

2 tbsp ground coriander

400 ml / ¾ pt / 1 ½ cups beef stock

125 g / 5 oz / ¾ cup dried apricots and dates, finely chopped

6 tbsp orange juice

10 ml / 2 tbsp clear honey

METHOD

- Heat the oil and fry the lamb cubes until brown and sealed. Set to one side.

- Add more oil and sauté the onion, herbs, spices and garlic for 3 minutes.

- Add the stock, honey and orange juice and zest and stir thoroughly. Bring gently to the boil. Add the potatoes, dates, apricots and simmer for 5 minutes.

- Place the spicy tagine sauce and lamb pieces into the slow cooker. Stir well and cook on a low setting for 8 hours.

- Serve hot with rice, couscous or pitta bread.

BEEF, POTATO AND LENTIL STEW

SERVES 6

PREPARATION TIME: 25 MINUTES
COOKING TIME: 8 HOURS

1 kg / 2 lb silverside beef, cut into 2 cm cubes

30 ml / 2 tsp vegetable oil

1 stalk celery, chopped

1 tbsp plain (all-purpose) flour

6 small carrots, scrubbed, trimmed and blanched for 5 minutes

1 courgette (zucchini) in ½ in slices

1 bay leaf

4 medium potatoes, peeled, quartered and blanched for 5 minutes

1 clove

2 tbsp fresh basil, finely chopped

1 x 400 g can of chopped tomatoes

1 onions, sliced

150 ml ¼ pt / ½ cup beef stock

salt and ground black pepper

GARNISH
fresh parsley

METHOD

• Heat the oil and fry (sauté) the beef cubes until brown and transfer to the slow cooker.

• Sweat the onions and vegetables for 5 minutes. Stir in the flour and cook for 1 further minute.

• Add the stock and tomatoes, clove and herbs to the pan and season.

• Transfer all the ingredients to the slow cooker with the herbs

• Cover and cook on a low setting for 8 hours.

• Taste and adjust seasoning

• Pour into a casserole dish before serving and sprinkle with parsley.

CRAYFISH AND BROCCOLI STEW

SERVES
4

PREPARATION TIME: 15 MINUTES
COOKING TIME: 4 HOURS 15 MINUTES

110 ml / 4 fl. oz / ½ cup olive oil

4 cloves garlic, minced

2 large heads of broccoli

4 large crayfish

675 g / 1 lb 8 oz / 4 ½ cups whole shrimp

250 ml / 9 fl. oz / 1 cup fish stock

30 ml / 1 fl. oz / 2 tbsp Cognac

55 ml / 2 fl. oz / ¼ cup double (heavy) cream

salt and pepper

METHOD

- Remove the florets from the broccoli and finely dice the stems.

- Chop the florets into small pieces, reserving 4 large ones for the garnish.

- Heat the olive oil in a large saucepan set over a moderate heat.

- Season the crayfish and sauté for 1–2 minutes, tossing and stirring occasionally.

- Remove from the pan and transfer to a slow cooker.

- Deglaze the pan with the Cognac and pour into the slow cooker.

- Add the fish stock, broccoli pieces and shrimp.

- Cook on a low setting for 4 hours.

- Pour in the cream after 4 hours and stir well.

- Adjust the seasoning to taste.

- Spoon into serving bowls and position the crayfish with the large pieces of broccoli in the centre of the dishes.

- Serve immediately.

LENTILS WITH CHICKEN

SERVES
4

PREPARATION TIME:60 MINUTES
COOKING TIME: 6 HOURS

4 chicken breasts, flattened between

30 ml / 1 oz / 2 tbsp olive oil

2 cloves garlic, minced

250 g / 10 oz / 1 cup chopped parsley

200 g / 8 oz / 1 cup orange lentils

750 ml / 1 pt 6 fl. oz / 3 cups stock

salt and pepper

CRUMB COATING

1 egg, lightly whipped

2 tbsp flour

150 g / 5 oz / ½ cup fresh breadcrumbs

3 tbsp vegetable oil

METHOD

- Wipe with oil and heat the slow cooker. In a pan, sweat the onion, parsley and garlic in the olive oil for 5 minutes. Drain off any juices.

- Cool slightly and spoon into each chicken breast before rolling up.

- Pour the lentils and stock into the slow cooker and cook for 2 hours on a medium setting.

- Place the chicken breasts, with the overlapping edge downwards, in the bottom of the slow cooker. Cook for a further 4 hours.

- Remove from the slow cooker and allow to cool.

- Dip each breast into the flour then dip into the whipped egg, and then the breadcrumbs. Set on a non-stick oiled baking tray.

- Drizzle the breasts with vegetable oil and cook in a hot oven set at 180°C (160°C fan) / 350F / gas 4 for 20 minutes until crisp and golden.

DUCK WITH CHERRIES

SERVES
4

PREPARATION TIME:20 MINUTES
COOKING TIME: 8 HOURS

1.75 kg / 4lb duck

30 ml / 2 tbsp goose fat

salt and pepper

cherry sauce

225 g / 8 oz / 1 cup de-stoned cherries

100 ml / 3 ½ fl. oz / ½ cup red wine

1 tbsp cornflour

1 tbsp red wine vinegar

1 tsp brown sugar

½ tsp cinnamon

METHOD

- Grease and warm the slow cooker. Wipe the duck with kitchen towel and prick the skin evenly with a fork. Rub salt into the skin.

- Heat the goose fat in a heavy pan and brown the duck all over. Stand to one side.

- To make the sauce, put all the sauce ingredients into a pan, except cornflour and vinegar Bring to a boil and place in the slow cooker. Sit the duck on top of the sauce and cover with the lid. Cook for 8 hours on a low setting.

- Preheat the oven to 200°C (180°C fan) / 400F / gas 6. Remove the duck carefully from slow cooker to avoid breaking it up and place on a baking tray. Roast it in the oven for 20 minutes to crisp the skin.

- Spoon off as much duck oil from the sauce as possible. Transfer the cherry sauce to a saucepan on the hob.

- Mix the cornflour with the vinegar and stir into the sauce. Bring to a simmer for a couple of minutes to thicken. Carve the duck and serve hot with the sauce.

CHICKEN CASSEROLE

SERVES
4

PREPARATION TIME: 25 MINUTES
COOKING TIME: 8 HOURS

1 x 4 lb chicken jointed

salt and freshly ground pepper

30 ml / 2 tbsp vegetable oil

1 tbsp butter

2 large garlic cloves, minced

¼ tsp Cayenne pepper

1 medium onion, finely chopped

4 sage leaves

2 tbsp bulgar wheat

1 tsp salt

60 ml / 2 oz / ¼ cup vodka

1 green pepper, thinly sliced

1 red pepper, thinly sliced

170 g / 6 oz cauliflower florets

170 g / 6 oz / 1 ½ cups mushrooms, quartered

500 ml / 1 pint chicken stock

100 ml / 4 fl. oz / ½ cup double (heavy) cream

GARNISH
chopped parsley leaves

METHOD

- Heat the butter and oil in a heavy based pan over a medium heat

- Add the onions and garlic and soften, then add chicken pieces and brown all over – add to the slow cooker.

- Add the sliced peppers and vegetables and stir well for 2 minutes

- Pour over the vodka, bulgar wheat and stock and bring to the boil. Add the herbs and spices.

- Pour the casserole into the slow cooker and cook for 6 hours on a low setting.

- Remove from the heat and stir in the cream.

- Taste and adjust seasoning

- Garnish with parsley leaves and serve.

FISH PEPPER STEW

SERVES
4

PREPARATION TIME: 20 MINUTES
COOKING TIME: 6 HOURS

500 g / 1 lb / 2 ½ cups mixed white fish
(eg. cod, haddock, coley)

1 x 400 g can pineapple chunks with juice

1 red pepper, cut into small cubes

2 tbsp korma curry paste or powder

2 tbsp vegetable oil

2 garlic cloves, minced

1 medium onion, finely sliced

1 pinch saffron soaked in 100 ml /
4 fl. oz / ½ cup chicken stock

1 tbsp cornflour (cornstarch) in 2 tbsp of
pineapple juice

50 ml / 4 fl. oz / ¼ cup plain yoghurt

½ tsp brown sugar

GARNISH
4 tbsp fresh parsley, chopped

METHOD

- Heat the oil in a pan and gently sauté the onion, garlic, peppers and korma paste for 5 minutes.

- Add the chicken stock, sugar and pineapple juice, less 2 tbsp and bring to the boil.

- Add the stew to the slow cooker, cover with the lid and cook for 6 hours on low.

- Transfer to a saucepan and bring to a simmer.

- Mix the cornflour (cornstarch) with the remaining 2 tbsp of pineapple juice, and stir into the stew gently to thicken.

- Spoon into serving dishes and garnish with the parsley and freshly ground black pepper.

- Serve warm alongside white rice.

BRAISED LAMB NECK WITH CARROTS

SERVES
6

PREPARATION TIME: 20 MINUTES
COOKING TIME: 2 HOURS

2 tbsp olive oil

6 lamb neck chops

1 onion, quartered and sliced

2 cloves of garlic, finely chopped

1 tsp cumin seeds

100 ml / 3 ½ fl. oz / ½ cup dry white wine

4 large carrots, peeled and sliced

400 ml / 14 fl. oz / 1 ½ cups vegetable stock

a few sprigs flat leaf parsley

salt and freshly ground black pepper

METHOD

• Preheat the oven to 180°C (160°C fan) / 350F / gas 4.

• Heat the oil in a large cast iron casserole dish. Season the lamb with salt and pepper and sear on both sides. Transfer to a plate and set aside.

• Add the onion, garlic and cumin to the pan and fry for 5 minutes over a low heat.

• Deglaze the pan with the wine and let it bubble until almost completely evaporated, then add the carrots and stock.

• Bring the liquid to the boil, then cover the dish and braise in the oven for 2 hours or until the lamb is very tender.

• Adjust the seasoning with salt and pepper and garnish with parsley before serving.

CURRIED CHICKEN CASSEROLE

SERVES
4

PREPARATION TIME: 15 MINUTES
COOKING TIME: 6 HOURS

4 tbsp sunflower oil

1 large chicken, cleaned and trimmed with wishbone removed

4 onions, cut into wedges

6 cloves garlic, peeled

4 bay leaves

2 tbsp Madras curry powder

2 tsp ground cumin

2 tsp ground coriander seeds

1 tsp ground paprika

1 tsp turmeric

METHOD

- Truss the chicken using kitchen string so that it is securely tied.

- Mix the ground spices with some seasoning in a small mixing bowl.

- Rub the chicken with some of the oil and sprinkle over half of the spice mixture, reserving the rest for a garnish.

- Heat a large frying pan or casserole dish over a moderate heat until hot.

- Seal the chicken until golden brown, then remove to a plate to one side. Reduce the heat and add the remaining oil.

- Brown the onions and garlic in the oil until soft. Transfer to a slow cooker and sit the chicken on top.

- Cover and cook on a medium setting for 6 hours.

- After 6 hours, test to see if the juices run clean when the thickest part of the thigh is pierced. If so, the chicken is ready.

- Spoon everything into a casserole dish.

- Garnish the top of the chicken with the remaining spice mixture and the bay leaves.

ROAST PORK WITH CINNAMON

SERVES
6

PREPARATION TIME: 10 MINUTES
COOKING TIME: 6–8 HOURS 10 MINUTES

30 ml / 1 fl. oz / 2 tbsp groundnut oil

1½ kg / 3 lb piece of pork knuckle,
washed and patted dry

4 cinnamon sticks

30 ml / 1 fl. oz / 2 tbsp balsamic vinegar

salt and pepper

METHOD

- Rub the pork knuckle with the oil and season generously.

- Heat a large frying pan over a high heat until hot.

- Seal the pork until golden brown in colour all over.

- Remove from the pan and place in a slow cooker.

- Add the cinnamon sticks and cover with a lid.

- Cook on a medium setting for 6–8 hours until the flesh is cooked.

- Once the flesh is cooked, baste in the vinegar before transferring the knuckle and any juices to a roasting dish for presentation.

PORK STEW

SERVES
4

PREPARATION TIME: 15 MINUTES
COOKING TIME: 8 HOURS 15 MINUTES

55 ml / 2 fl. oz / ¼ cup sunflower oil

900 g / 2 lb pork cheek, trimmed and diced

2 large globe artichokes, trimmed and sliced

1 onion, very finely chopped

1 clove of garlic, minced

500 ml / 18 fl. oz / 2 cups ham stock

salt and pepper

2 tbsp flour

150 g / 5 oz / ½ cup fresh breadcrumbs

3 tbsp vegetable oil

GARNISH

2 tbsp parsley leaves

METHOD

- Heat the sunflower oil in a large casserole dish set over a moderate heat until hot.

- Season the pork and seal in batches until golden brown in colour all over.

- Move each sealed batch to a slow cooker when done.

- Add the sliced artichoke, stock, onion and garlic and stir well.

- Cover with a lid and cook on a low setting for 8 hours until the pork is starting to fall apart.

- Adjust the seasoning to taste before spooning into serving dishes.

- Serve immediately.

DUCK WITH PINEAPPLE

SERVES
4

PREPARATION TIME:10–15 MINUTES
COOKING TIME: 6 HOURS 10 MINUTES

30 ml / 1 fl. oz / 2 tbsp sunflower oil

4 duck legs, trimmed

2 tbsp honey

600 g / 1 lb 5 oz / 3 cups canned pineapple chunks, drained

500 ml / 18 fl. oz / 2 cups chicken stock

1 star anise, crushed

salt and pepper

METHOD

• Heat a casserole dish over a moderate heat until hot.

• Coat the duck legs in the oil and honey and season generously.

• Seal in the casserole dish until golden brown all over before moving to a slow cooker.

• Add the pineapple, stock, star anise and seasoning and stir well.

• Cover with a lid and cook on a medium setting for 6 hours until the duck legs are cooked through.

• Adjust the seasoning to taste before spooning into serving dishes. Carve the duck and serve hot with the sauce.

VEGETARIAN

ROASTED PALM HEARTS

SERVES
4

PREPARATION TIME: 10–15 MINUTES
COOKING TIME: 4 HOURS 25 MINUTES

55 ml / 2 fl. oz / ¼ cup olive oil

10–12 palm hearts, trimmed

2 limes, juiced

small handful of basil leaves, finely chopped

salt and pepper

GARNISH

2 limes, cut into wedges

sprigs of flat-leaf parsley

METHOD

- Place the palm hearts in a large mixing bowl and combine with half of the olive oil, half of the lime juice and some seasoning.

- Toss well to coat in the mixture before moving to a slow cooker.

- Cover with a lid and cook on a low setting for 4 hours until softened.

- Once done, remove from the slow cooker and pat dry.

- Preheat the oven to 190°C (170°C fan) / 375F / gas 5.

- Arrange the palm hearts on a roasting tray and coat in the remaining olive oil, adding more seasoning.

- Roast for 12–15 minutes until lightly coloured.

- Remove from the oven and toss with the remaining lime juice and the chopped basil.

- Arrange on serving plates and garnish with slices of lime and sprigs of parsley before serving.

VEGETABLE TAGINE

SERVES
4

PREPARATION TIME: 5 MINUTES
COOKING TIME: 3 HOURS 30 MINUTES

2 tbsp olive oil

1 onion, finely chopped

2 large carrots, peeled and cubed

2 large parsnips, peeled and cubed

1 tbsp fresh root ginger, finely chopped

3 cloves of garlic, finely chopped

1 tsp ras el hanout spice mix

250 ml / 9 fl. oz / 1 cup vegetable stock

12 prunes, halved and stoned

salt and freshly ground black pepper

pre-cooked couscous

GARNISH
sprig of mint

METHOD

• Preheat the oven to 140°C (120°C fan) / 275F / gas 1.

• Heat the oil in a large wok set over a moderate heat.

• Sauté the onion, carrots, parsnips, ginger and garlic for 3–4 minutes, stirring frequently.

• Stir in the ras el hanout, then pour in the stock and bring to the boil.

• Pour the contents of the pan into a tagine. Cover with the lid and cook in the oven for 3 hours.

• Stir the prunes into the tagine. Increase the oven to 190°C (170°C fan) / 375F / gas 5 and return to the oven, uncovered, for 15 minutes or until the prunes are just tender.

• Season to taste with salt and pepper before serving with couscous.

OMELETTE STEW

SERVES
4

PREPARATION TIME: 10–15 MINUTES
COOKING TIME: 4 HOURS 35 MINUTES

FOR THE OMELETTE

55 ml / 2 fl. oz / ¼ cup olive oil

3 large potatoes, peeled and finely diced

1 onion, finely chopped

6 large eggs

250 ml / 9 fl. oz / 1 cup whole milk

salt and pepper

FOR THE STEW

30 ml / 1 fl. oz / 2 tbsp olive oil

1 onion, finely chopped

4 cloves of garlic, minced

400 g / 14 oz / 2 cups canned chopped tomatoes

250 ml / 9 fl. oz / 1 cup passata

½ tsp caster (superfine) sugar

salt and pepper

METHOD

- Prepare the stew by heating the olive oil in a large saucepan over a medium heat. Sweat the onion and garlic for 5 minutes.

- Add the sugar, chopped tomatoes, passata and seasoning and stir well. Pour into a slow cooker and cook for 4 hours on a low setting.

- Turn the slow cooker off and preheat the oven to 180°C (160°C fan) / 350F / gas 4.

- Line a round cake tin with greaseproof paper. Heat the olive oil in a casserole dish over a medium heat. Sweat the onion and potato for 8–10 minutes.

- Meanwhile, whisk together the eggs, milk and seasoning in a bowl. Spoon the potato mixture into the base of the cake tin.

- Pour over the egg mixture and bake for 15–20 minutes. Remove from the oven and reheat the stew.

- Spoon the stew into serving dishes and turn the omelette out from the tin.

- Sit in the stew and garnish the dishes with the parsley.

CAJUN TOFU STEW

SERVES
4

PREPARATION TIME: 15 MINUTES
COOKING TIME: 4 HOURS

2 tbsp groundnut oil

300 g / 10 ½ oz / 2 cups tofu, cubed

2 large carrots, peeled and cubed

400 g / 14 oz / 2 cups canned kidney beans,
drained and rinsed

2 sticks celery, sliced

110g / 4 oz / 1 cup lumache pasta

1 red pepper, deseeded and finely diced

2 sheets dried seaweed, cut into strips

250ml / 9 fl. oz / 1 cup vegetable stock

2 tbsp dark soy sauce

GARNISH

2 tbsp flat-leaf parsley, finely chopped

4 sprigs of flat-leaf parsley

METHOD

- Heat the groundnut oil in a large wok set over a moderate heat.

- Sauté the carrot, pepper, celery and tofu for 3–4 minutes, stirring frequently.

- Spoon into a slow cooker and add the pasta, kidney beans, seaweed and stock.

- Cover and cook on a medium setting for 4 hours.

- Adjust the seasoning to taste after 4 hours using the soy sauce.

- Spoon into serving bowls using a slotted spoon and garnish with a sprinkle of chopped parsley as well as a sprig of parsley leaves before serving.

VEGETABLE AND PEAR CASSEROLE

SERVES
4

PREPARATION TIME: 25 MINUTES
COOKING TIME: 6 HOURS

30 ml / 2 tbsp sunflower or olive oil

1 medium onion, peeled and sliced in circles

1 garlic clove, crushed

2 carrots, roughly chopped and blanched
for 5 minutes

1 celery stick, chopped

100 g / 4 oz sweet potato sliced

100 g / 4 oz salsify, peeled and sliced

100 g / 4 oz shredded Savoy cabbage

100 g / 4 oz cauliflower florets

1 tbsp tomato purée

4 beef tomatoes, skinned and sliced

3 tbsp cider vinegar

150 ml / 5 fl. oz / ½ cup dry cider

2 tbsp parsley, chopped

150 ml / 5 fl. oz / ½ cups vegetable stock

2 conference pears, cored and quartered

salt and black pepper

METHOD

- Blanch all the hard vegetables for 5 minutes, drain and dry.

- Heat the oil in a pan and gently sweat the onions, garlic, and all the vegetables and pear pieces.

- Add the vinegar, stock, tomato paste, herbs and cider and bring to the boil for 5 minutes.

- Place casserole into the slow cooker and cook on medium for 6 hours.

- At the end of cooking, taste and add salt and black pepper as required.

- Spoon into serving dishes and garnish with chopped parsley.

MUSHROOM AND VEG STEW

SERVES
4

PREPARATION TIME: 25 MINUTES
COOKING TIME: 6 HOURS
60 ml / 2 fl. oz / 4 tbsp olive oil
2 garlic cloves, crushed
2 carrots, sliced and blanched
4 large beef tomatoes, quartered
2 potatoes, cubed and boiled
700 g / 1 ½ lb mixed mushrooms
1 tbsp thyme, chopped
2 bay leaves, crushed
½ tbsp oregano, chopped
½ tbsp parsley, chopped
salt and black pepper to taste
700 ml / 1 ½ pt / 3 cups vegetable stock

METHOD

- Heat the oil in a large wok or heavy pan and sauté all the vegetables, herbs and garlic.

- Add the stock, tomatoes and seasoning and bring to the boil for 5 minutes.

- Pour all the ingredients into the slow cooker and cook on medium for 6 hours to allow flavours to infuse.

VEGETABLE CASSEROLE

SERVES
4

PREPARATION TIME: 10 MINUTES
COOKING TIME: 6 HOURS

330 ml / 1 fl. oz / 2 tbsp sunflower or olive oil

2 medium onions, sliced

2 garlic cloves, crushed

100 g / 4 oz cauliflower florets

400 g / 14 oz / 2 cups canned tomatoes, chopped

4 beef tomatoes, skinned and sliced

2 green and 2 red peppers, sliced

1 tbsp chilli pepper

1 tsp oregano

300 ml / 10 ½ fl. oz / 1 ¼ cups vegetable stock

salt and black pepper

METHOD

- Heat the oil in a pan and gently sweat the onions and garlic for 5 minutes stirring regularly.

- Mix in the chilli pepper and stir for 2 minutes.

- Pour in the canned tomatoes and add the sliced beef tomatoes, cauliflower, peppers and oregano.

- Pour in the vegetable stock and bring to the boil.

- Place casserole into the slow cooker and cook on medium for 4 to 8 hours.

- At the end of cooking, taste and add salt and black pepper as required.

- Spoon into serving dishes and garnish with chopped parsley.

STEWED VEGETABLES WITH SAGE

SERVES
4

PREPARATION TIME: 15 MINUTES
COOKING TIME: 4 HOURS

4 tbsp olive oil

2 large red peppers, deseeded and chopped

300 g / 10 ½ oz / 2 cups parsnips, peeled and quartered

300 g / 10 ½ oz / 2 cups carrots, peeled and quartered

2 tbsp flaked (slivered) almonds, lightly toasted

handful sage leaves

3 sage leaves, cut chiffonade

METHOD

- Combine the parsnips and carrots in a large mixing bowl.

- Add the olive oil and seasoning and toss well.

- Heat a large frying pan set over a moderate heat until hot then pan-fry the carrots and parsnips for 3–4 minutes until lightly coloured, tossing and stirring occasionally.

- Transfer the contents of the frying pan to a slow cooker and add the peppers and the sage leaves.

- Cook on a medium setting for 4 hours until the vegetables are soft and tender.

- Spoon into serving bowls using a slotted spoon and garnish with the finely sliced sage and almonds before serving.

VEGETARIAN CHILLI CON CARNE

SERVES
4

PREPARATION TIME: 20 MINUTES
COOKING TIME: 4 HOURS

500 g / 1 lb vegetarian mince

1 tbsp vegetable oil

½ tsp salt

1 large onion, finely chopped

1 red pepper, chopped

1 tsp hot chilli (chili) powder (or mild chilli powder if preferred)

1 tbsp paprika

2 tsp cumin

1 tsp oregano

3 garlic cloves

2 tbsp tomato purée

1 x 400 g can tinned chopped tomatoes

150 ml / 5 fl. oz / ¾ cup water

1 vegetable stock cube

½ tsp sugar

1 x 400 g red kidney beans cooked

METHOD

- Sauté the onions, garlic and pepper until soft. Add the chilli, paprika and cumin, stir well and cook for a further 4 minutes.

- Add the vegetarian mince and brown thoroughly.

- Pour over the water, sugar, oregano, tomatoes and purée. Crumble in the stock cube and stir thoroughly.

- Transfer to the slow cooker.

- Cover and cook on a high setting for 3 ½ hours.

- Drain the kidney beans and stir into the chilli con carne. Replace lid and cook for a further ½ hour.

- Serve immediately with rice or grated cheese and tortilla chips.

VEGETABLE STEW

SERVES
4

PREPARATION TIME: 30 MINUTES

COOKING TIME: 4 HOURS

900 g / 2 lb mixed / 8 cups vegetables, diced
(can include carrot, turnip, swede, cauliflower,
broccoli, courgette, pumpkin, wild mushrooms,
potatoes etc) all finely diced

60 ml / 4 tbsp vegetable oil

5 g / 1 tsp cumin seed

15 g / 1 tbsp flour

1 l / 35 fl. oz / 4 cups vegetable stock

10 ml / 2 tsp white wine vinegar

2 garlic cloves, minced

1 x 400 g can chickpeas (garbanzo beans), drained

METHOD

- Heat the oil in a pan and gently sauté all the vegetables, cumin seeds and garlic for 10 minutes stirring gently.

- Add the flour to the pan and stir in for a further 3 minutes.

- Add the stock and vinegar mixing well. Bring to the boil.

- Transfer to the slow cooker, cover with the lid and cook for 4 hours on medium.

- Add the chickpeas and stir. Cover the pan and slow cook for 15 minutes.

- Spoon into serving dishes.

VEGGIE BOUILLABAISSE

SERVES
4

PREPARATION TIME: 10–15 MINUTES
COOKING TIME: 4 HOURS 20 MINUTES

55 ml / 2 fl. oz / ¼ cup olive oil

4 fennel bulbs, trimmed and chopped

1 leek, sliced and washed

4 carrots, peeled and sliced

2 large white potatoes, peeled and diced

1 tbsp tomato purée

1 tsp saffron threads, infused in the stock

500 ml / 18 fl. oz / 2 cups vegetables stock

400 g / 14 oz / 2 cups canned chopped tomatoes

salt and pepper

GARNISH

sprigs of basil leaves

1 tbsp picked thyme leaves

METHOD

- Heat the olive oil in a large saucepan set over a medium heat until hot.

- Sweat the fennel, leek, potato and carrots for 8–10 minutes, stirring occasionally until softened.

- Add the tomato purée and stir well, then add the stock and chopped tomatoes with some seasoning.

- Stir well before pouring into a slow cooker.

- Cover with a lid and cook on a medium setting for 4 hours until the vegetables are soft.

- Adjust the seasoning to taste before ladling into serving bowls and garnishing with a sprinkling of thyme leaves and a sprig of basil.

VEGETABLES WITH TURMERIC

SERVES
4

PREPARATION TIME: 15–20 MINUTES
COOKING TIME: 4 HOURS 15 MINUTES

4 tbsp olive oil

55 ml / 2 fl. oz / ¼ cup olive oil

1 large courgette (zucchini), cut into ribbons using a vegetable peeler

2 large carrots, peeled and cut into ribbons using a vegetable peeler

2 large beef tomatoes, sliced

2 onions, sliced

2 cloves of garlic, minced

1 aubergine (eggplant), halved and sliced

1 tsp ras el hanout

1 tsp turmeric

1 tbsp honey

250 ml / 9 fl. oz / 1 cup vegetable stock

salt and pepper

GARNISH
small handful of picked flat-leaf parsley leaves

METHOD

- Heat some of the olive oil in a large casserole dish set over a moderate heat.

- Sauté the vegetables in batches for a few minutes each, apart from the tomato.

- Use fresh oil for each batch and move each completed batch to a slow cooker when done.

- Add the tomato slices to the slow cooker once all the vegetables have been sautéed.

- Add the ground spices, honey and seasoning and stir well.

- Cover with the stock and cover with a lid.

- Cook on a medium setting for 4 hours.

- Adjust the seasoning to taste after 4 hours and transfer to serving dishes using a pair of tongs.

- Garnish with the parsley leaves before serving.

FISH

SQUID STEW

SERVES
4

PREPARATION TIME: 15 MINUTES
COOKING TIME: 4 HOURS

125 ml / 4 ½ fl. oz / ½ cup olive oil

450 g / 1 lb baby squid tentacles

450 g / 1 lb octopus tentacles, chopped

4 red onions, chopped

2 spring onions (scallions), sliced

1 red pepper, deseeded and chopped

1 tbsp oyster sauce

1 tsp hot sauce

1 lime, juiced

GARNISH

150 g / 5 oz / 1 cup tuna steak, diced

½ courgette (zucchini), cored and finely sliced

2 green chilli (chili) peppers

4 sprigs of basil leaves

METHOD

- Heat some of the olive oil in a large wok over a moderate heat until hot.

- Stir-fry the squid for 1 minute then transfer to a slow cooker.

- Add some more oil and stir-fry the octopus for a minute before adding to the slow cooker.

- Add more of the oil and stir-fry the spring onion, leek and red pepper for a few minutes.

- Stir in the oyster and hot sauce as well as the lime juice.

- Pour the contents of the pan into the slow cooker and cook on a high setting for 4 hours.

- Adjust the seasoning to taste after 4 hours and spoon into a balti dish.

- Garnish with the courgette, chilli peppers and basil sprigs before serving.

SWORDFISH WITH TOMATOES

SERVES 4

PREPARATION TIME: 10 MINUTES
COOKING TIME: 4 HOURS

2 tbsp olive oil

4 x 225 g / 8 oz swordfish steaks

4 onions, sliced

4 cloves garlic, sliced

4 tomatoes, deseeded and sliced

2 orange peppers, deseeded and sliced

1 yellow pepper, deseeded and sliced

2 tsp ground coriander seeds

2 tsp ground cumin

1 tsp ground cinnamon

½ tsp paprika

1 tbsp honey

250ml / 9 fl. oz / 1 cup warm water

2 tbsp coriander (cilantro), roughly chopped

2 tbsp chervil leaves, finely chopped

GARNISH

4 sprigs of coriander (cilantro)

METHOD

- Rub the swordfish steaks with the olive oil and season generously.

- Heat a large griddle pan over a moderate heat until hot.

- Seal the swordfish in the pan for a few minutes on both sides until marked.

- Move to one side as you prepare the vegetables.

- Add the onions and garlic to the pan and sauté for a few minutes.

- Transfer the onion and garlic to a slow cooker.

- Add the peppers and tomato to the pan and sauté for a few minutes, tossing occasionally.

- Add to the slow cooker along with the ground spices and honey.

- Stir well then sit the swordfish steaks on top.

- Pour in the warm water, cover and cook on a medium setting for 4 hours.

- Adjust the seasoning to taste after 4 hours, before spooning the vegetables and swordfish into serving bowls.

- Sprinkle the chopped herbs on top and garnish with sprigs of coriander before serving.

TUNA CASSEROLE

SERVES
4

PREPARATION TIME: 15 MINUTES
COOKING TIME: 5 HOURS 15 MINUTES

45 ml / 1 ½ fl. oz / 3 tbsp sunflower oil

600 g / 1 lb 5 oz piece of tuna steak, cut in half

300 g / 10 ½ oz / 4 cups closed cup mushrooms, sliced

2 onions, finely sliced

2 large carrots, peeled and finely diced

250 ml / 9 fl. oz / 1 cup vegetable stock

250 ml / 9 fl. oz / 1 cup water

salt and pepper

GARNISH

2 tbsp picked chervil leaves

2 tbsp parsley leaves

METHOD

- Coat the tuna steak in the oil and season well.

- Heat a large frying pan over a high heat until hot and seal the tuna until golden brown in colour all over.

- Remove to a slow cooker and reduce the heat under the frying pan a little. Add the onions, mushrooms and carrot and sauté with a little salt for 5 minutes, stirring occasionally.

- Spoon into the slow cooker and add the stock and water.

- Stir well before covering and cook on a medium setting for 5 hours until the tuna is just cooked through.

- Remove the tuna from the slow cooker and spoon the vegetables into serving dishes using a slotted spoon.

- Sit the tuna on top and garnish with chervil.

ROASTED ANISEED BASS

SERVES
4

PREPARATION TIME: 10 MINUTES
COOKING TIME: 3–4 HOURS 15 MINUTES

125 ml / 4 ½ fl. oz / ½ cup olive oil

2 medium sea bass, gutted and cleaned

1 lemon, sliced

1 tbsp caraway seeds

1 tsp mustard seeds

4 red peppers, deseeded and sliced

150 g / 5 oz / 1 cup pitted green olives, sliced

150 g / 5 oz / 1 cup sun-dried tomatoes, roughly chopped

1 tbsp aniseed

salt and pepper

METHOD

- Heat half of the olive oil in a large casserole dish set over a medium heat until hot.

- Sauté the peppers, olives and sun-dried tomatoes with the aniseeds for 2–3 minutes, stirring occasionally. Add half of the caraway and mustard seeds and stir well before spooning into a slow cooker.

- Make three slashes in one side of each sea bass and stuff with the lemon slices.

- Sit the sea bass on top of the vegetables in the slow cooker and cover with a lid.

- Cook on a medium setting for 5–6 hours until the sea bass is cooked through and the flesh is firm yet slightly springy to the touch.

- Discard the aniseeds and carefully remove the sea bass.

- Spoon the vegetables and olives into a serving dish and sit the bass on top before garnishing with the remaining caraway and mustard seeds.

FISH TAGINE

SERVES
4

PREPARATION TIME: 20 MINUTES
COOKING TIME: 5 HOURS 20 MINUTES
75 ml / 3 fl. oz / ⅓ cup olive oil
2 large grey mullet, gutted and cleaned
450 g / 1 lb / 3 cups new potatoes, halved
2 yellow peppers, deseeded and sliced
2 cloves of garlic
500 ml / 18 fl. oz / 2 cups fish stock
125 ml / 4 ½ fl. oz / ½ cup dry white wine
½ tsp saffron threads, infused in the stock
1 tsp ras el hanout (Moroccan spice blend)
1 tsp paprika
½ tsp Cayenne pepper
salt and pepper

GARNISH
sprigs of coriander (cilantro) leaves

METHOD

- Cut the mullet into 2 in thick steaks.

- Coat in most of the oil and season well.

- Heat a large casserole dish over a moderate heat until hot and seal the fish until golden in colour all over.

- Remove to a slow cooker and reduce the heat under the dish a little.

- Add the remaining oil and sauté the peppers and garlic for a few minutes, stirring frequently.

- Add the ground spices, stir well, add the wine, stock and potatoes.

- Pour into the slow cooker and cover with a lid.

- Cook on a medium setting for 5 hours until the fish is cooked through.

- Adjust the seasoning to taste before ladling into serving dishes.

- Garnish with coriander before serving.

ROASTED RED MULLET

SERVES
4

PREPARATION TIME: 10-15 MINUTES
COOKING TIME: 4 HOURS 15 MINUTES

125 ml / 4 ½ fl. oz / ½ cup olive oil

2 red mullet, gutted and cleaned

450 g / 1 lb / 3 cups vine cherry tomatoes,
vine removed

500 ml / 18 fl. oz / 2 cups fish stock

2 shallots, finely sliced

salt and pepper

FOR THE PURÉED FENNEL

55 g / 2 oz / ½ stick unsalted butter

4 fennel bulbs, trimmed and sliced

250 ml / 9 fl. oz / 1 cup whole milk

salt and pepper

GARNISH

2 sprigs of rosemary

METHOD

- Rub the outside of the mullet with oil and season.

- Combine the shallot, tomatoes, stock, remaining oil and seasoning in a slow cooker. Sit the red mullet on top and replace lid.

- Cook on a medium setting for 4 hours until the fish is cooked.

- Prepare the fennel by melting the butter in a saucepan set over a medium heat.

- Sweat the fennel for 10 minutes, stirring occasionally until softened.

- Cover with milk and cook for 20 minutes at a gentle simmer.

- Strain and spoon the fennel into a food processor.

- Add a little cooking milk and purée until smooth; add more milk if too dry.

- Cover and chill until ready to serve.

- Pour everything from the slow cooker into a roasting dish and preheat the oven to 190°C (170°C fan) / 375F / gas 5.

- Place in the oven for 10 minutes.

- Spoon the purée onto a plate and garnish.

- Remove the red mullet from the oven and garnish before serving.

MONKFISH IN GARLIC

SERVES
4

PREPARATION TIME: 10 MINUTES
COOKING TIME: 5 HOURS

4 tbsp cup olive oil

900 g / 2 lbs monkfish tail

6 sprigs of thyme

6 cloves garlic, lightly crushed

1 tsp black peppercorns

METHOD

- Heat half of the olive oil in a large frying or fish pan over a moderate heat until hot.

- Rub the monkfish tail with the remaining olive oil and season generously.

- Seal the monkfish until golden brown.

- Remove from the pan and add the peppercorns and cloves of garlic, sautéing them in the oil for a minute.

- Spoon them into the slow cooker and sit the monkfish on top.

- Cook in the slow cooker on high for 5 hours until the monkfish is firm and is starting to come away from the tailbone.

- Spoon everything back into a metal roasting pan.

- Garnish with the sprigs of thyme before serving.

OCTOPUS AND CHICKPEA STEW

SERVES
4

PREPARATION TIME: 10 MINUTES
COOKING TIME: 6 HOURS

3 tbsp olive oil

200 g / 7 oz / 1 cup chickpeas (garbanzo beans), soaked in water overnight then drained

1 octopus, roughly chopped

2 medium white potatoes, peeled and cut into small chunks

500ml / 18 fl. oz / 2 cups vegetable stock

2 tsp paprika

1 tsp ground cumin

1 lemon, juiced

GARNISH

pinch smoked paprika

handful frisée lettuce

METHOD

- Heat the olive oil in a large frying pan set over a moderate heat.

- Sauté the octopus with the lemon juice, ground cumin, paprika and seasoning for a few minutes, stirring occasionally, before transferring to a slow cooker.

- Add the potatoes, chickpeas (garbanzo beans) and stock and stir well.

- Cover and cook on a low setting for 6 hours.

- Adjust the seasoning to taste after 6 hours and stir through the frisée lettuce.

- Spoon into serving dishes and garnish with pinches of smoked paprika before serving.

TUNA CIVET

SERVES
4

PREPARATION TIME: 20 MINUTES
COOKING TIME: 5 HOURS

4 tbsp olive oil

675 g / 1 lb 8 oz tuna loin

1 onion, finely chopped

1 clove garlic, minced

150 g / 5 oz / 1 cup pancetta, cut into lardons

150 g / 5 oz / 1 cup pearl onions, peeled

300 g / 10 ½ oz / 2 cups Charlotte potatoes, peeled

125ml / 4 ½ fl. oz / ½ cup red wine

GARNISH

2 sprigs tarragon, chopped

2 tbsp picked chervil leaves

2 tbsp parsley leaves

METHOD

- Wrap the tuna loin tightly in film and roll into a cylinder. Refrigerate overnight. The next day, unwrap from the film and tie with kitchen string at 1 inch intervals.

- Rub with half of the olive oil and season well. Heat a pan and seal the tuna until golden in colour all over.

- Place in a slow cooker. Reduce the heat under the frying pan and add the remaining olive oil.

- Sauté the pancetta for 2–3 minutes, stirring frequently, then add the onions and potatoes.

- Cook for a further 3 minutes, then deglaze the pan with the red wine. Pour the contents of the pan over the tuna in the slow cooker.

- Cover and cook on a low setting for 5 hours. Adjust the seasoning to taste after 5 hours then spoon onto a serving dish. Garnish with the tarragon and some ground pepper before serving.

GROUPER WITH FENNEL

SERVES
4

PREPARATION TIME: 20 MINUTES
COOKING TIME: 4 HOURS

2 tbsp olive oil

4 225 g / 8 oz grouper steaks, pin-boned

4 fennel bulbs, trimmed and chopped

1 preserved lemon, sliced

2 cloves garlic, minced

2 tomatoes, cored and diced

450 g / 1 lb / 3 cups white potatoes, peeled and cut into chunks

125ml / 4 ½ fl. oz / ½ cup dry white wine

500ml / 18 fl. oz / 2 cups fish stock

2 bay leaves 2 star anise

salt and pepper

METHOD

- Heat the olive oil in a large frying pan set over a moderate heat until hot.

- Season the grouper and flash-fry for 30 seconds on both sides before moving to a slow cooker.

- Add the fennel, preserved lemon, garlic, tomato and potato and reduce the heat a little.

- Sauté for 4–5 minutes, stirring occasionally.

- Add the white wine and let it reduce by half before pouring everything into the slow cooker. Add the stock and bay leaves and stir carefully.

- Cover and cook on a medium setting for 4 hours.

- Adjust the seasoning to taste after 4 hours and ladle into serving bowls.

- Serve immediately.

FISH CASSEROLE

SERVES
4

PREPARATION TIME: 20 MINUTES

COOKING TIME: 6 HOURS

4 tbsp olive oil

4 sea bass fillets, pin-boned

300 g / 10 ½ oz / 2 cups whole prawns (shrimps)

450 g / 1 lb / 3 cups clams, cleaned

55g / 2 oz / ⅓ cup chorizo, finely sliced

250ml / 9 fl. oz / 1 cup dry white wine

250ml / 9 fl. oz / 1 cup fish stock

4 tomatoes, cored and sliced

4 cloves garlic, minced

1 fennel bulb, trimmed and finely chopped

1 tbsp flat-leaf parsley, roughly chopped

METHOD

• Heat the olive oil in a large casserole dish set over a moderate heat.

• Add the clams and half of the white wine and cover with a lid.

• Remove the dish from the heat after a few minutes and shake well with the lid in place.

• Strain the clam liquid into a slow cooker and discard any clams that haven't opened.

• Place the clams, sea bass, prawns, tomatoes, fennel, garlic, chorizo, stock and remaining wine in the slow cooker.

• Stir gently a few times and cover with a lid.

• Cook on a low setting for 6 hours until the seafood is cooked through.

• Adjust the seasoning and stir in the chopped parsley.

• Spoon into serving bowls and serve immediately.

FISH STEW

SERVES
4

PREPARATION TIME: 20 MINUTES
COOKING TIME: 4 HOURS

4 tbsp olive oil

450 g / 1 lb red mullet fillets, pin-boned

225 g / 8 oz sea bass fillets,
pin-boned

225 g / 8 oz / 2 cups mussels

4 whole prawns (shrimps), peeled and de-veined

4 tomatoes, cored and cut into wedges

2 cloves garlic, minced

2 tbsp Cognac

250ml / 9 fl. oz / 1 cup double (heavy) cream

250ml / 9 fl. oz / 1 cup fish stock

1 tsp saffron threads, infused in the stock

GARNISH
4 sprigs basil leaves

METHOD

- Heat the olive oil in a large frying pan set over a moderate heat until hot.

- Season the fish fillets and flash-fry with the garlic for 1 minute.

- Transfer to a slow cooker.

- Add the prawns (shrimps) and mussels and flash-fry for a minute as well before transferring to the slow cooker.

- Deglaze the pan with the Cognac before reducing the heat and adding the infused stock and cream.

- Stir well and pour into the slow cooker.

- Add the tomatoes and cover with a lid.

- Cook on a medium setting for 4 hours.

- Adjust the seasoning to taste after 4 hours.

- Ladle the broth and seafood into serving bowls.

- Garnish with sprigs of basil leaves before serving.

SICILIAN-STYLE TUNA

SERVES
4

PREPARATION TIME: 15 MINUTES
COOKING TIME: 4 HOURS

4 tbsp olive oil

450 g / 1 lb tuna steak, diced

2 onions, sliced

2 large potatoes, peeled and finely diced

2 carrots, peeled and finely diced

400 g / 14 oz / 2 cups chopped tomatoes

250ml / 9 fl. oz / 1 cup vegetable stock

125ml / 4 ½ fl. oz / ½ cup dry white wine

110g / 4 oz / 1 cup peas, frozen or fresh

METHOD

• Heat the olive oil in a large casserole dish set over a moderate heat until hot.

• Season the tuna and flash-fry in batches before moving to a slow cooker.

• Reduce the heat under the dish and add the onions, potatoes, carrots and a little seasoning.

• Sauté for a few minutes, stirring occasionally, before deglazing with the white wine.

• Let it reduce by half before adding the stock, chopped tomatoes and peas.

• Pour into the slow cooker and cover with a lid.

• Cook on a medium setting for 4 hours.

• Adjust the seasoning to taste after 4 hours before spooning into a baking dish for presentation.

• Serve immediately.

SPICY ROAST TUNA POT

SERVES
6

PREPARATION TIME: 20 MINUTES
COOKING TIME: 4 HOURS

1 kg / 2 ½ lb fresh tuna fillet

15 ml / 1 tbsp vegetable oil

1 star anise, whole

¼ tsp chilli (chili) flakes

3 spring onions (scallions) finely chopped

100 g / 4 oz porcini mushrooms, sliced

2 tbsp mixed Italian herbs

4 garlic cloves, minced

1 bay leaf

1 tsp ground coriander

½ tsp ground cloves

1 x 400 g can chopped tomatoes

80 ml / 2 ½ fl. oz / ⅓ cup white wine vinegar

salt and ground black pepper

GARNISH
fresh basil

METHOD

• Pre-warm the slow cooker.

• Heat the oil and fry (sauté) the tuna fillet. Add the cloves, coriander, garlic, a little salt and some ground black pepper to the tuna and turn regularly until brown all over, leave to one side.

• In the pan, heat the tomatoes, chilli flakes, star anise, onions, herbs, bay leaf, cloves and white wine vinegar for 5 minutes and place into the slow cooker.

• Sit the tuna fillet on top and scrape any ingredients remaining in the pan around the tuna.

• Cover with the lid and cook on a low setting for 4 hours for a rare finish to the fish.

• Taste and adjust seasoning.

• Serve tuna with the sauce spooned over and garnished with fresh basil.

INDEX